## INTRODUCTION
**GOOD ART FORCES US TO ASK OURSELVES QUESTIONS. IT CHALLENGES OUR ASSUMPTIONS AND OPENS US UP TO NEW IDEAS.**

Bad art, surprisingly, does something even more magical.

It makes us envision the artist, the person who sat in a studio or workshop or Walgreen's parking lot for hours and created something. Who was this jerk? What kind of big, dumb, unskilled idiot were they?

It's easy to imagine the artists like this, blindly punching a canvas with a brush, all slavering jowls and dead eyes. But I don't think it's fair to say the unknowns in our collection are without spirit. None of these works are boring, none of them are uninspired. They have a zest to them, a resolve. A fear to face the Inevitability of Failure and sit down with it for a cup of tea.

I'm sure many of these artists thought their paintings were "bad", too. But they persevered and finished them. They fought the terror of failure—that primal fear we all share, that makes all of us want to give up, want to take the easy road—they fought that fear with every single brushstroke, thumbtack, and hammerfall. They finished what they started.

And that beautiful flower of humanity bore for us a deformed fruit. Take a bite, won't you? *~ David Cairns, Artologist*

## UNTITLED WITH MOON, 1992
*Materials: Acrylic on bus transfers*

Created during the artist's relapse phase, this work was rescued from a thrift store and painstakingly restored with forensic dish soap to its present condition. It is unclear why the painting has an unsettling orange cast. Some believe the artist wished to deface the work. Others believe the painting was abandoned in a garage where water damage took its toll. Regardless, the stain lends a certain patina to the work that only adds to its allure. Wait, no it doesn't.

*~EDW Lynch, Art Collector*

# MICHAEL JACKSON/MERMAN

ALEJANDRO DE BUN BUN, 1987

*Materials: Watercolor and pencil on paper*

Literally some people have viewed this work and wondered: is that Michael Jackson? And also: Where is his right arm? These and other questions have plagued scholars for years. For the exotic sea beast pop singer figure we see here is truly one of the art world's great mysteries.

~EDW Lynch, Art Collector

## NO EXPLANATIONS.
## NO ANSWERS.
### 'ANONYMOUS'

*Materials: pastels, colored pencils, Some Kind of Paint, Um a Heavyish Posterboard?*

This piece was rendered by the famed nonsense artist 'Anonymous.' "Forget the form," she (?) said in a letter to the Academy of Art University Admissions Review Board, "Look at this painting and then try to forget what you're looking at. Remember that your eyes always lie, and try to 'see' past them. Imagine that rather than looking, your eyes are drunk and they are DESCRIBING a dream that they once heard someone explaining to a bored friend in a Thai restaurant. Also included are my favorite food and prime number down there in the corner."

*~David Cairns, Artologist*

## MESS, 3RD NON-ATTEMPT
GEORGE RR CRUMB
*Materials: Thickly-applied oils, Nutella™, caulk*

'Mess' is best accompanied by this note from the artist:

"I originally painted 'Mess' after ingesting a large amount of pot-cupcakes [Ed. note: 'cupcakes' is a slang term for LSD or 'acid'] and eating my friend Jessica's pussy. Turned out later she had V.D. Anyway, I thought it was a terrible painting, so I threw it away. A couple months later, I tried to do a still life of a fish taco and produced the same exact painting. I don't remember painting it. It's like I was in a fugue state. Anyway, it was still a terrible painting so I did a couple shots of Scope to take the edge off and threw away the canvas. The following week I did a painting of the ocean -- it was really beautiful, seriously -- and then I passed out. When I woke up and this painting was on my easel. I was going to throw it away for, I guess at this point, the third time, but by then it had grown on me."
*~David Cairns, Artologist*

## A TOUCHY POET
## & A MODEST LOVER
JEROME DOSTOYEVSKY
*Materials: AntiFreeze, boot black, JPEG compression artifacts*

This piece reminds the viewer of the responsibility Western society places on us to control nature through the means of technology. Depicting a wild, culturally barren 'wilderness," the artist has built a train track and an electric power line through it, dividing it into two smaller, more manageable wildernesses, the dichotomy representing the duality of Man. A 'locomotive' (literally: 'crazy movement') patrols the border between the two worlds. The fox ('intellect') tries to hide behind a bush, but her technological overlords see all.
*~David Cairns, Artologist*

## MARIA
QUINTIN RODRIGUEZ, 2006
*Materials: Watercolor and pencil on paper*

This haunting portrait seems to draw us deep into the eyes and grimacing but perfect teeth of Maria Shriver. We sense the veil of artifice surrounding Shriver, the tug of fame, the tragedy of the spotlight. But mostly we can't look away from those eyes and those white, white teeth.
*~EDW Lynch, Art Collector*

## PORTRAIT OF UNCLE GLEN
## -- THANKSGIVING, 1983
ALVAREZ HICKENLOOPER
*Materials: Canvas, watercolors, cadaver eyebrow hair*

One in a series of captivating family portraits, "Uncle Glen" is nothing less than a shocking comment on the deterioration of the American family. The subject, his collar spread wide like the legs of his many conquests, has the cold hard stare of a silver fox who has run out of henhouses to plunder. After a rude remark about cousin Judith's abortion, he is on the receiving end of a vicious potato peeler attack, leaving his handsome face bloodied. The whole scene, like the curtains in the background, is ugly.
*~ Spencer Bainbridge, Art Historiologian*

# HAIL MARY FULL OF ANGELS

IGNACIO KORNBLUTH, 1998

*Materials: Acrylic on Bible pages*

The Virgin Mary is beset by a swarm of angels in this tribute to Italian Renaissance fresco by Ignacio Kornbluth. The curiously upright stance of the inverted angel on the lower right of the painting allows the work to be enjoyed upside-down.
*~EDW Lynch, Art Collector*

## MIDDAY CONTEMPLATION WITH CAT
REBA SMATHERS

*Materials: Watercolor on canvas with Fancy Feast stains, some spit*

"Nature," wrote the great naturalist John Muir, "is the most natural thing there is." Muir's eloquence rings true more than a century later, and his writings no doubt inspired this reflective masterwork. Kipling himself could not have imagined a more peaceful friendship between man and beast. The man's very pinkness, his naked innocence, suggests a long and complicated symbiotic partnership. The cat is bored, but cats are annoying, so what do you expect? Muir said that too.
*~Spencer Bainbridge, Art Historiologian*

## CRAFTER'S OUTLET ANYONE CAN PAINT #28
M. HARMON, 1990

*Materials: Acrylic on paint by numbers card*

The artist created this work during his controversial Paint By Numbers period of the late 1980s and early 90s. A raccoon engages the viewer with his coal black eyes, caught in the act of posing for a painting.
*~EDW Lynch, Art Collector*

## MURKY LAKE DURING THE ORANGE DAYS
GEOFFREY LEMONBAR, 1985
*Materials: Oil on 50% recycled consumer content*

Mountain peaks climb into a chemical fog in this intriguing landscape painting. To the left we see a majestic generic conifer rendered in the artist's peculiar let's-use-all-the-paint brushstrokes. There's a message in the tree, something in the brushstrokes and the muddy colors. And that message is "Goddamnit."
*~EDW Lynch, Art Collector*

## STILL LIFE OF A FLYING WHALE (WITH JELLYFISH)
*Materials: Light, oil-based paints, the first time using LSD*

The artist's own misconceptions about the form of whales and their method of locomotion is evident in this piece, but he cleverly illustrates how freeing not knowing anything about the subject can be. Here we see a whale free from all normal, expected, natural (and therefore trite) context. It has transcended the place in the universe it was given. It has grown horns, it is friends with jellyfish. It can fly.
*~David Cairns, Artologist*

## GYNECOMASTIC OCTOGENARIAN BLUES
### KEFFIR MCMARTENSEN
*Materials: small nylon brush, Crayola™ SuperPaintz™ 10-pack*

The vase that is the subject of 'Gynecomastic Octogenarian Blues' calls to mind tragedy in all its forms. Where once the vase was whole, now it has a breach in its side. The artist explores this theme with the jagged edge's detailing, but also reminds us that no tragedy or setback is ever insurmountable. The rays of light shining through the gaping hole illustrate the figurative and literal silver lining of proverb. The growth of green reinforces this--the natural world (and hence the universe itself) never stops growing and changing, despite human affairs.

The image is rendered with a quaint forced perspective that takes the viewer out of their initial interpretation, and reminds them that objectivity is the key to overcoming an existential crisis. Your Lucky numbers are: 12, 17, 35, 86, 12.
*~David Cairns, Artologist*

## FISSURE DA PLAYA
### DIONOFFRIO P'STA
*Materials: #1 Pencil, #3 Pencil, colored pencil, tissue paper,*
*Cardboarda di Firenze*

This French New Wave sketch is unique in the sense that it can be considered both pre- and post-Primitivist. There are two subjects in this piece –– the house in the distance and the cracked earth in the foreground. The house itself represents the traditional family structure of the Classical era. Its dilapidation and the cracked, barren earth that surrounds it epitomize the Primitivist idea that people live in different ways. The selection of medium and mode was intended to enhance the house's plainness, and is itself Expressionistic.
*~David Cairns, Artologist*

## THE ARCH OF CHRONOS & OTHER SYMBOLS
### LIONEL ONDRY
*Materials: Very dry blue paint #3, a hard flat horsehair brush*

'The Arch…' transports the viewer to a land that is both familiar and unfamiliar, a place of realistic fantasy. The deep ravine has been dug out by a muddy river, representing the inexorable passage of time, and, by extension, the viewer's own mortality. The ram is a symbol of vitality. It is ever watchful of the steady progress of time, wearing us down. The titular arch itself is a reminder: where once we were a full, high mountain, now time has taken all but the memory of our greatness.
*~David Cairns, Artologist*

## FLOWERS (UNTITLED)
LARDSON CREEME
*Materials: canvas, oils, frame, matting, frame*

Scholars know nothing about the origins of this piece or its creator, aside from the contents of the hand-written autobiography that was found lying next to it. This mystery has engendered the piece with significant intrigue; with some art historians insisting it must be a lost original Rembrandt, and others a high school student's art class project. Consequently, the piece has been sold at auction numerous times, at prices alternating between the tens of millions and "like twelve bucks."

*~David Cairns, Artologist*

**TEQUILA SUNRISE**
SCOTT NICHOLSON, 1974
*Materials: Tequila, grenadine,
orange juice, canvas*

Pour Tequila and orange juice in
a glass filled with ice. Add grenadine. Do not stir.
*~EDW Lynch, Art Collector*

**ON THE FARM**
IRMA WAWAWAM, 1982
*Materials: Acrylic on tear-soaked canvas*

This piece presents dystopian vision of agrarian existence shrouded in the post-modern kitsch of the cow-on-the-farm genre. The cow in this instance is clearly an avatar for mankind and the tyranny of life in a world ruled by technology. Look carefully at his eyes. His *human* eyes. Shudder.
~EDW Lynch, Art Collector

## NOT A YELLOW TRUMPET
### SUZANNE CARAVAGGIO, 1999
*Materials: Acrylic on #8 Art Board*

Created over the course of one and a half hours, this elegiac painting speaks volumes to the artist's vague knowledge of guitar appearance and function. The piece was found on a curbside in San Francisco by art expert and humanitarian EDW Lynch. It would look nice on a yellow wall or in a black dumpster.
*~EDW Lynch, Art Collector*

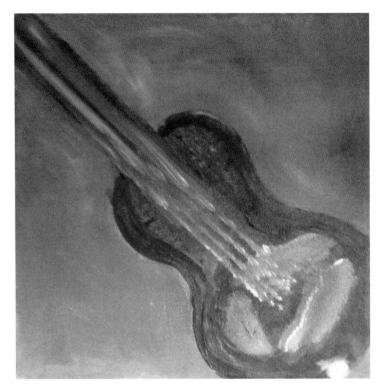

## FISH / MILITARY SPACECRAFT
### RYAN REYNOLDS
*Materials: Body oil paints, crayon*

The artist here has represented herself as a simple golden fish set on a simple blue background. However, the observer's eyes are distracted by the coil of supine serpents that bethrong it. What purpose do they serve? Do they represent hardship, or does the artist just like dark, oily swirly-wirlies?
*~ David Cairns, Artologist*

## THE PRINCE-BISHOP OF TEMESCAL
RFE LINSTLER
*Materials: I got a staple in my finger what do I do*

'The Prince-Bishop' is a self portrait in the traditional Wagonerian style, in which the artist depicts himself in a disguise or otherwise peculiar clothing, especially clothing of another culture. Though a truly traditional example of this style has the subject looking dead into the viewer's perspective, this artist has opted for a coy look to the side, leaving the viewer to question 'Why?' Is it cowardice or gentility? Is he trying to think of a lie?
*~David Cairns, Artologist*

## SEEMS LIKE A NICE DAY!
ELVIS NORMAL
*Materials: simple canvas, pastels, Stereolab CD*

'Seems Like a Nice Day!' is a complicated piece. While it is technically a "drawing," it also evokes (perhaps even more strongly than its visual elements) the sounds and smells of a marshy beach. In order to truly appreciate this piece, the 'viewer' should stand a shoulders distance from it and close his or her eyes, then bend forward slightly and inhale deeply the scent of the canvas. A recording of seagulls will accentuate underscore the sensation, as will putting sand in one's shoes [NOT PROVIDED].
*~David Cairns, Artologist*

## WADING TO EXHALE
DR. JABO BRONTLEY
*Materials: Extra-thick Office Depot brand paper, colored pencils (half sharpened)*

Brontley, once a professor of animal husbandry at Yuma Vocational College, described this piece as "a nightmare of post-postmodern self-image." The central figure, a bather both infantile and buxom, shows a heartbreaking reluctance to become fully submerged, having been filled with insecurity by the harshness of modern society. The figures in the background are predatory and cactus-like for some reason. Dr. Brontley is currently single.
*~Spencer Bainbridge, Art Historiologian*

## CAW CAW CAW I MEAN PAINTING
LISA "HAWKY" NOTABIRD
*Materials: Assorted Inks, grey rainwater, "How to Draw Technophobic Nightmares" by H.R. Giger, bleached parchment*

The artist asks us to imagine a world in which birds (and presumably other animals) have developed their own technology. Would they be better at it than humans? Such deconstruction of man's technological achievement exaggerates how 'un-human' our actual inventions are. Will we ever be able to 'wear' an 'iPod'? Probably not, but, then, why would we want to?
~David Cairns, Artologist

-------
## CAROLYNE NOONE
*Materials: Bits of charcoal, Sweet 'n' Savory Dry Ink Rub, Stipple Sauce #9, CD of Sublime's '40 Oz. To Freedom'*

In this piece, the artist represents her inner frustration. The lack of any brilliant hue silently demands the viewer's eyes to pass over the piece in a gallery, almost as if to say, "Don't look at me, I'm not worth your time." The artist has depicted herself as a skull, bald of all flesh, which is a symbol of her raw appetite (note the teeth) for success (note the lack of success).
~David Cairns, Artologist

## LAMPREY BARBIE
### CYLBILL LAMPLIGHT

*Materials: Crayola™ Rockin' Blue™ #9 Magic Marker™, Sharpie™ felt-tip #6, pastel, canvas*

The deep blue palette of Lamprey Barbie lulls the viewer into the piece, drawing them closer. The bright white eye attracts one's attention like the light of a lamprey eel. The viewer finds themselves coaxed into the painting, lost in the forbidden dark of the deep sea of their mind. And then they can look at it.

*~David Cairns, Artologist*

## JUST CAUSE
### BERNERD T. SIGHS

*Materials: Two (2) canvaseses, light oils, mixed tedia*

Through this piece and its companion "um sure?" (a four-hundred-foot-long triptych, currently on display at the Royal Art Museum of the Justification in Saskatoon, Saskatchewan, Canada), the artist begs the question, "like, what?" This piece is a classic example of the Undisciplinari-ast school, which came in to and fell out of prominence in Toronto in the third week of November, 1998.

*~David Cairns, Artologist*

## SELF PORTRAIT: JORGE JETSON
### FRENCH RAINBOW
*Materials: Medium-grade acid-full paper, water colors paints, water, Colgate™ WhiteGuard™ Toothpaste*

This piece depicts the hazy silhouette of a floating cityscape, a rendering of our possible future, à la Bespin. But: it is only visible through a smoky, gloppy patina. The artist asks, 'What is the environmental cost of the Cloud City?' and, furthermore, 'Why would we want one?' Truly, a stirring piece for adults and children of all ages.
*~David Cairns, Artologist*

## PAINTING FROM SUNDAY AFTERNOON, NOVEMBER 24TH, 1991
DR STEVE KNOTTS, DDS
*Materials: Level 3 Landscape Painter's Starter Pack, particle board frame*

The history of art can be traced back from student to teacher, movement to movement, following the same arc of the rest of human history, constantly tracing the details of events and moods in Humanity's ever-shifting, ever-evolving zeitgeist. So many artists never take on an apprentice, and so their style, their depth of knowledge and technique, terminate with the artist's death. Few great artists, however, take on millions of students, as did the late Bob Ross.

Because of Mr Ross's tireless dedication, the art world was infused with a tidal wave of incredibly derivative, similarly bland, boring landscapes, thus sinking the price of art to where the common man can now appreciate it in his or her own home. After Bob Ross, a piece by Rembrandt or Cezanne can now be had for only seventy or eighty dollars. Most no longer even remember when such pieces would fetch prices into the millions.
*~David Cairns, Artologist*

## DOWN, DOWN, DOWN: FIERCE
### KEYWAN TRAN-SPORT
*Materials: just some papers, markers, purple stuff, what else*

'Down, Down, Down: Fierce' reflects the artist's inner monster, and subverts his relationship with it—What if the monster were on the outside? This post-modern take on Magical Realism incorporates elements of cubism and Super Street Fighter III Turbo.
*~David Cairns, Artologist*

-----
## C. HHHHHHHHHH
*Materials: Dry Brush, Gasoline, Primer*

This simple landscape isn't even a landscape at all -- it's a painting. And it is a painting only in the most literal sense. It was once a blank canvas, which then had paint applied to it. The paint dried in the shape of a snowy mountain crag, by all accounts the simplest, smallest idea that a painting can express. There is absolutely no artistic expression in this piece; it is regarded as a piece of art solely because it is hanging in a gallery. The context is essential, the piece cannot stand on its own and retain this label. As soon as this piece is removed from a gallery, it might as well be a piece of WonderBread™ for all the significance it has.
*~David Cairns, Artologist*

## FLAMINGO (C)
R. KAYE
*Materials: Oil on matte paper*

Though harshly derided by some critics -- the word "pukey" reappears time and again -- Kaye's work is among the most ubiquitous in the contemporary art world. Prints of this piece, from Kaye's "Birds of Paradise" series, has been featured in some of the country's worst hotels and best rest stops. Daringly, Kaye has eschewed a traditional color palette in favor of mustardy hues, reminiscent of an autumn sunset, but also mustard. Kaye has more money than you will ever have, but try not to think about it.
*~Spencer Bainbridge, Art Historiologian*

## #5: HARRY AND THE SHIRT FROM KOHL'S
### ROSEANNE LEAVEY
*Materials: Canvas, pastels, Hai Karate aftershave*

Roseanne Leavey first attracted notice in the Pittsburgh art scene with her daring series re-imagining famous cinematic creatures as humans in everyday life. "#1: Godzilla at Trader Joe's" is perhaps the best known piece, along with "#7: Gremlin Teleconference." This selection shows Harry, of "Harry and the Hendersons," stripped of his Sasquatch persona. His trepidation is plain to see in his haunted eyes. He is contemplating his new role as a part of the race that shunned him, his confusion at the modern world, and whether he made the right decision becoming a high school guidance counselor.
*~Spencer Bainbridge, Art Historiologian*

## A SUNNY AFTERNOON EVERYONE IS WATCHING
J. "REVELER" HEINZ
*Materials: Heavy oils, little plastic owl doodles, little plastic parrot doodles, fake flowers,*

San Francisco has long been a "vital" part of drug culture in the United States and the world, due to the popularization of psychedelics and hallucinogens in the city in the 1960s. For decades, young "artists" have followed the footsteps of their heroes, flocking to the Haight Ashbury district to sleep in the park and bother people for money while under the influence of mind-"expanding" drugs. This piece is an homage of sorts to this very lifestyle. We can see a number of people dressed ridiculously, bothering one another and hawking dirty bits of paper, while the giant painterly flowers grow out of nothing in particular. Viewers are encouraged to experience this piece in all the senses they can muster. Get up close to it. Put your nose in the vestibule, smell the carefully-crafted street people. If one closes one's eyes, one can almost hear them say, "Green herb. Dank bud here."
*~David Cairns, Artologist*

## STILL LIFE WITH BLUE VASE
JULI BEGALFI
*Materials: Drafting paper, watercolors*

Look at this. The flowers look so nice, like real flowers only better because they won't die. My favorite is the little one who's all droopy. I mean, he's down, but he's not out, you know? I just... I just don't know what to say other than it's beautiful and pretty and that's enough sometimes. I'm not going to lie: I've been drinking.
*~Spencer Bainbridge, Art Historiologian*

## AWAITING THE RETURN (SNACKTIME IN TOLEDO)
ARLENE SMOKLER

*Materials: canvas, watercolors, Burt's Bees lip balm*

Jesus, upon his crucifixion, swore he'd return to walk the earth again. Two millennia later, an androgynous senior citizen waits patiently for the Nazarene to fulfill his promise. His/her edges are blurred to signify the grace which radiates from the most loyal of Christ's followers. The red polka dot sofa sprouts spectral wings, symbolizing Jesus' ascension to heaven all those years ago. And the uneaten, oversized Bugle snack treat, literally dripping with tasty goodness, represents the hunger for answers that burns inside the faithful.
~Spencer Bainbridge, Art Historiologian

## BARTLEBY WITH THE NORTHERN LIGHTS
JOHANN GRUMMLER-DANST
*Materials: wood, oils*

The Aurora Borealis dances in the night sky, but not for Bartleby. The subject is believed to be a representation of the artist's brother, a simpleton who never removed his plumed hat except during lovemaking, when he put on a larger hat. His complete obliviousness to the wonders of the cosmos, combined with his effeminate shoulder bag, suggest a deep, heavily feathered eccentricity. It also appears as if someone has stolen his shopping cart.
*~Spencer Bainbridge, Art Historiologian*

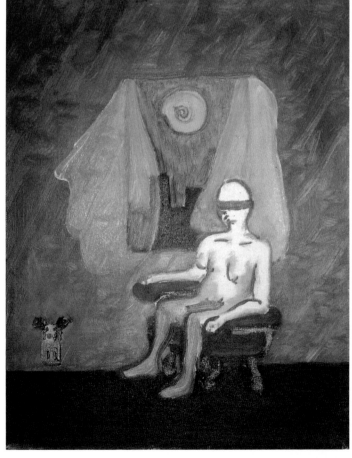

## HUMDONGER
DOUG TOLFTVÄAELD
*Materials: Canvas, oils, Viagra, the world's most flattering mirror*

The artist paints herself as a dog pretending to be a man on a hot Summer evening in New York City. The cocktail of amphetamines and hallucinogens starting to take hold, she straps herself to a chair to protect her fragile, imaginary penis from the walls' melting into the evening's sky, where the Sun gains consciousness, finding itself more marshmallow Peep than it is accustomed to being. She blindfolds herself against the mäelström of things realizing things.
*~David Cairns, Artologist*

# DEATH IN REPOSE (SUMMER RERUNS)

ALEXANDRA MCNICHOLAS

*Materials: Canvas, oils, Puffy Paints*

Death does indeed, from time to time, take a holiday. This piece finds the Reaper himself enjoying a "staycation" of the most mundane sort. The very banality of this activity, or lack of activity, conjures a sense of macabre irony; we are always mindful of Death's presence in our lives, and Death never misses an episode of "The Glee Project." The raven, perched on the Reaper's left shoulder, also watches but does not comprehend. Ravens are stupid.

*~Spencer Bainbridge, Art Historiologian*

## HIPSTER CHRISTENING
### M.A. HOAREHOCK
*Materials: Canvas, mixed oils, nightmare tonic, whatever*

This piece recalls the artist's own traumatic Christening / Bris / parents' divorce. The parents, undeniably hip, look down at their pathetic prodigy, their hopes and dreams for him suddenly stillborn, they realize that a Christening ceremony is not "ironic," even with a Little Person as officiant.
*~David Cairns, Artologist*

## EVERYTHING I DO (I DO IT FOR YOU)

MERKHOPFER BLUM

*Materials: Canvas, oils, a poor understanding of human anatomy*

There is nothing greater than the transformative power of love. In this piece, Blum presents two lovers transmogrified by their passion. Afro at full, glorious flower, the man has reverted to a reptilian state of carnal hunger, his forked tongue feeling around for some moist reciprocation, or perhaps just a nosh. The woman, unable to satisfy her lust with two human hands, extends nine greedy tentacles. She closes her eyes in anticipation. At last, she sighs, Internet dating has proven effective.

*~Spencer Bainbridge, Art Historiologian*

## WHAT
RICKY LAKE
*Mat-he-rials: charcoal, sulphur, man-made heavy cardstock, a real man's course hungry blood*

Late anti-feminist painter / essaying / poet / "dick-sculptor" Ricky Lake, most famous for not being the popular daytime television host, made this painting on a dare. While the artist is a pretty generally hated person, this piece is notable for having popularized the highlighting of a woman's "tee tees and coo-joo" while not depicting the man's "bongo mallet." While initially seen as juvenile, these terms have since become commonplace.
~*David Cairns, Artologist*

## REVENGE OF ZOROASTER
### GRENADINE HAMBURGER
*Materials: paint, time, space, hope, fear*

The Bible tells the parable of the Garden of Eden, wherein the Serpent convinces Eve to eat of the Tree of Knowledge, teaching her the difference between Good and Evil and freeing Humankind of the manacles of its innocence -- an affair known as Original Sin. Themes of this story are the basis of nearly all cultures descended from Abrahamic religions, composing all of Western society. The artist, heavily influenced by "Chicken Soup for the Country Soul" and then "The Five-Day Study Bible," figured they would give it a shot, and try to hit everything at once. With polka dots.

*~David Cairns, Artologist*

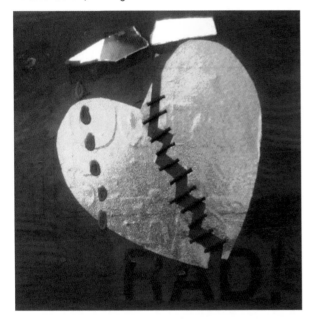

## RAD: A LIE MADE TO A BEGGAR
### BRIAN CHERGHORN AKA "THE UNKNOWN ARTIST"
*Materials: Lettermatic RI-84 letterpress machine, gold leaf, Kirkland Felt Blood Drops*

Why does heartbreak always make us cry? Why wouldn't it make us bleed or pee or defecate? Why not yell quasi-anachronistic expressions? Literature theorists have long said there is no reason for it. Richard Longview, eminent Harvard chair of Comparative Literature Theory, has even said, "there is no reason for it!" And yet it still holds true, unwavering and unchanging. Perhaps someday, Humankind will learn how to break this terrible cycle of oracular leakage, but until then, the only cure is ice cream.

*~David Cairns, Artologist*

## SATURDAYS WITH MR. ALBERT
BRAM HARDWICKE
*Materials: Cardboard stock, Crayola Washables*

Perhaps Hardwicke's most accessible work, "Saturdays with Mr. Albert" shows little of the artist's usual flair for the bizarre. Clearly inspired by the cozy Americana of Norman Rockwell, it portrays a placid weekend visit with a beloved old relative. One can practically smell the fresh-baked cookies and lemonade. Despite this, most people seem to fixate on the naked transsexual in the bowler hat slaughtering the green demon.
*~Spencer Bainbridge, Art Historiologian*

# UNTITLED
## LULA WHODREW

*Materials: Memories, mixed media, a synapse, a book on Queer Theory, Jane Fonda Workout, VHS*

A number of images intermix here with varying effectiveness, and in their own way, form a sort of visual staccato. Like a John Cage arrangement operating without a conductor, the symbols in this piece present themselves just how they are, with no sense of preparation or aesthetic effort. In this sense, it is art at its purest, an expression of the artist's true sentiment, far before they consider whether it might be "good" or "make sense."
*~David Cairns, Artologist*

## RASPBERRY DREAMS NO. 14
WARREN DROULLIARD
*Materials: Oil and nightmares on recycled sympathy cards*

Darwin springs from the earth, like the glorious fauna he studied in the Galapagos. Is it the reincarnation of the Father of Modern Science, or just a red-hued likeness? It might be Santa. Anyway, he has a beard (Droulliard was famously inept at drawing upper lips). The sickly homunculus stands next to him, a symbol of evolution gone amok, tighty whiteys clinging on for dear life. He beckons to a lover or a sandwich. Both? Droulliard committed suicide shortly after this work, which makes the rainbows extra depressing.
*~Spencer Bainbridge, Art Historiologian*

## SPRING COLLECTION - BROOME STREET JACKET
CATHRAIN BRIPPLEBERRY
*Materials: Oils, "The Kiss" 26"x20" poster by Gustav Klimt, Fall 1999 JC Penny catalogue*

This illustration was commissioned for the Kate Spade catalogue in 2001. In producing this piece, the artist employed her oft-never-imitated process of eating other works of art, in an attempt to infuse her body and mind with her inspirations. Unfortunately, the artist was unaware of how bodies work. This illustration was never was never used in any advertisement.

Ms Brippleberry died in 2002 of ink poisoning.
*~David Cairns, Artologist*

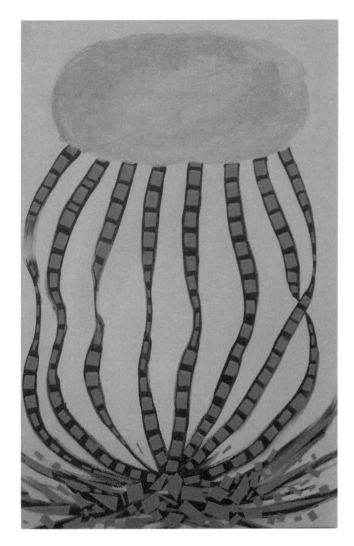

## REMEMBRANCE OF A REMINDER
KILROY SEQUINS-TURNIP
*Materials: Rock (crushed up into a fine dust, then mixed with an emulsifier to create paint)*

This is a depiction of the birth of Andrew WK, long considered by the 'Expression' community the herald of a third wave of living your life in an interesting way. The depiction is highly symbolic: the sun giving birth to rolls of film, which clatter and smash on the ground as would a disco mirror ball. The artist is essentially saying 'Disco is dead', 'Film is a medium without a message', 'The sun created everything', all sorts of stuff. Andrew WK is depicted on the back of this painting, but please don't look there, as he's invisible.
*~David Cairns, Artologist*

## A QUIET NIGHT IN THE SPACE GARDEN / DREAMHAZING
MILF TANDOORI
*Materials: Chalks, Longing*

This piece by the late proto-neo-feminist illustrator Milf Tandoori was, sadly, the last he created before tragically choking on a book of his own poetry in front of a captive audience at the S. Tokyo Sin Garden Gallery Bar & Grille in Minneapolis, Missouri. The rester dreams a dream about sleep and fails to spot the seahorse and tribal tattoo drawing the rester's finger into the water. The rester sleeps, wetter with the liquid of the subconcious. The friends patiently await the rester to pee him-/herself.
*~David Cairns, Artologist*

## THE NIGHT WE MET, SLOWLY FADING
### JOYCE HAROLD BATES
*Materials: Oils, scrapbook, patience*

Here, the artist, 107-years-old, recalls her fondest remaining memory, a sort of patio? Or a common area? I'm not sure, I think it was in Italy, but anyway there was this, this common area, and there was a staircase and a couple of, what are they called, plants!, there were a couple of plants, I remember, and that was where I met your father. It was in Germany, that's it, Germany. It was there and I -- actually, I think maybe I was a little girl. Yes, I hadn't met your father yet. This must have been when he was still living with his aunt and uncle on Long Island, before we both grew up and before, wait, no, it's the inside of that Olive Garden we went to in Tampa Bay in 2006. You remember, the nice one.
*~David Cairns, Artologist*

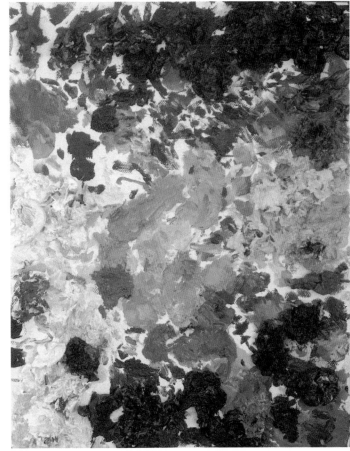

## HENRY KISSINGER - 34/237
### LADY KENNIFER L'PRINGLESALAD
*Materials: Heavy Oils, the Sweat of 400 college freshmen*

This is the thirty-fourth of a two-hundred-thirty-seven-piece polyptych of renderings of pop depictions of paintings of a blemish on Henry Kissinger's nose by famed New Neo-Renaisscientist Kennifer L'Pringlesalad. L'Pringlesalad was a founding member of the "Directorial Collectivist" school, which concerned itself with meta-productions of meta-media. In her multi-step process, her team of "expert" (novice) "artists" (unpaid interns) created a hand-drawn animation of Henry Kissinger lancing a blemish on his face. They then rendered extreme close-ups of each cell of the animation. If the viewer squints, they can see the imagine of Kissinger, tongue askance, carefully lancing the offending follicle, and, in the background, then-President Richard M. Nixon about to strike his dog Checkers.
*~David Cairns, Artologist*

## DESSERT'ED
### MATILDE HAND

Using various colored cake frosting stolen from a Safeway bakery, this piece engages the viewer almost immediately, challenging one to let go of rationale for just a moment, and fully absorb its striking symbolic symbols. The cherubic, cream-filled Rush Limbaugh hovers serenely above a sinister figure, severely tanned and yet a wisp of a man, whilst a ghost rushes in behind both figures, as if bursting with exciting news from its previous life, the asymmetrical rainbow binding all of them together.
~*Alani Foxall, Visual Consumer*

## YOU'RE KILLIN' ME, BRO
### CHUCK FONTES

A bromantic comedy gone so hellishly wrong, addict sports gambler and half-Naga Chuck Fontes' auto-biographical masterpiece depicts not just the exquisite pain of a Latin man's stranglehold but also having no shoulders. In an homage to Munch, Fontes desperately faces the audience while agony floods his every goateed pore, but his captor listens not, staring with empty satisfaction into yonder abyss, or perhaps at the basketball game on TV. I'm just surprised "benefit" is spelled correctly.
~*Professional Painting Yelper Ari Rust*

## IT'S MY ART, DAD!
ALAN L'NALHAL

This piece is indicative of the style of mid-2000s Portland dwellers, of trying to reinvent new ideas of what it could mean to be 'weird' or 'abstract' -- and finally found its home in the phrase 'totally whoa,' which so captured the movement, it became eponymous. Artists of the Totally Whoa style are characteristically very jaded, seeking only to produce that which has never been produced before, at the cost of the thing having any inherent meaning. The artist here depicts himself as a surprisingly well-rendered wolf, staring at the viewer dolefully, almost as if to say, "I hope you don't enjoy this, because nothing has meaning."
~David Cairns, Artologist

**MISSION B.A.G. (BAD ART GALLERY)**
*Occasionally Presented at*
518 VALENCIA
SAN FRANCISCO, CALIFORNIA

Only the finest bad art from esteemed Bay Area
collections (thrift stores, yard sales, flea markets)
presented in a ritzy Inner Mission gallery with
enlightening (and hilarious) catalog notes.

*Brought to you by SF IndieFest, sfindie.com*

*This book has been lovingly designed by
Annie Maley, gringostarr.com*

Made in the USA
Charleston, SC
09 December 2013